Queens and Princesses

Helen
OF TROY

by Sheila Griffin Llanas

Consultant:
Dr. Laurel Bowman
Department of Greek and Roman Studies
University of Victoria
Victoria, British Columbia

Capstone
press

Mankato, Minnesota

Snap Books are published by Capstone Press,
151 Good Counsel Drive, P.O. Box 669, Mankato, Minnesota 56002.
www.capstonepress.com

Library of Congress Cataloging-in-Publication Data
Llanas, Sheila Griffin.
    Helen of Troy / by Sheila Griffin Llanas.
        p. cm. — (Snap books. queens and princesses)
    Includes bibliographical references and index.
    Summary: "Describes the life of Helen of Troy" — Provided by publisher.
    ISBN-13: 978-1-4296-2308-7 (hardcover)
    ISBN-10: 1-4296-2308-X (hardcover)
    1. Helen of Troy (Greek mythology) I. Title.
BL820.H45L55 2009
292.1'3 — dc22   2008027661

Editor: Megan Peterson
Book Designer: Bobbi J. Wyss
Set Designer: Juliette Peters
Photo Researcher: Wanda Winch

Table of Contents

1 A NIGHT
That Changed
HISTORY

Fresh from her bath, Queen Helen of Sparta opened her ivory jewelry box. She chose a gold necklace with an **amethyst** stone. She slipped coiled gold bands around her arms and bangles on her wrists. That night, Helen and her husband, King Menelaus (men-uh-LAY-us), would entertain a prince from Troy. Helen wanted to look her best.

Helen's servants rubbed her arms and feet with perfumed oil. The oil made her skin shiny and soft. They curled and oiled her long hair to make it glisten. Then they pinned her hair with ivory combs high on her head, away from her face. Her glossy ringlets fell down her back in amber waves. For a royal touch, she wore a gold headband covered in jewels.

Helen's great beauty was known throughout ancient Greece.

amethyst — a type of quartz crystal that is purple or violet

Finally, Helen slipped into layers of long, woven robes that fell to the floor. She always prepared carefully for an evening feast. Sometimes she spent all day in her chambers getting ready.

The prince from Troy was named Paris. Although the Spartans and the Trojans were rivals, Paris came to Sparta as a friend. When he arrived, the royal throne room was filled with guests. They ate the best foods the palace could offer. Guests dined on chickpea pancakes, lentil stew, roast meats, fresh fruit, honey, and figs. The hall was bursting with music and dancing.

Helen often attended such fancy events. She had been Queen of Sparta for many years and a princess from birth. Helen entered the hall that night looking like a goddess. She smelled like roses. When she moved, her bangles and earrings rang together like musical chimes. Her sandals clattered on the stone floor.

Menelaus and Paris sat in silver-studded thrones at the front of the hall. They watched Helen glide across the floor and take her seat. Helen then turned to meet the handsome stranger, a man who would change her life, and history, forever.

Servants helped Helen bathe, dress, and put on makeup.

FACT OR FICTION?

Homer was the first to write about Helen.

Helen's story comes from the Mycenaean period (1550–1100 BC) of late Bronze Age Greece. During this period, the ancient city-state of Mycenae was the cultural center of Greece.

In Bronze Age Greece, people had a system of writing that historians call Linear B. The Greeks used it to keep accounts and lists of supplies. Historians have been unable to find letters, books, or diaries written using Linear B. There is no recorded history of that time period. What is known about Helen comes mainly from *The Iliad* and *The Odyssey*. These poems were written by an ancient Greek poet known as Homer. Homer wrote these famous poems around 700 BC, 500 years after Helen would have lived. He wrote his poems to tell the story of the Trojan War. The war ruined Troy and caused the deaths of many heroes. Helen's story is also revealed by historic clues from pieces of decorated pottery, **artifacts**, and ruins.

Historians have no proof that Helen actually existed. Stories about her are a major part of Greek literature and culture. Helen has puzzled people throughout the ages. Her story offers a glimpse into the life of a Bronze Age queen.

artifact — an object used in the past that was made by people

A ROYAL
Childhood

Helen was born in Sparta around 1200 BC. Helen's parents were King Tyndareus (tin-DARE-ee-uhs) and Queen Leda (LEE-duh) of Sparta. Sparta was a wealthy city-state in ancient Greece. Mountains surrounded Sparta, which helped protect the city.

As a princess, Helen's days were filled with riches beyond compare.

According to Greek mythology, Zeus was the king of all gods.

AN UNUSUAL BIRTH

The ancient Greeks believed gods ruled the earth, sea, and sky. People built temples and prayed to the gods for protection. According to legend, Helen's real father was Zeus (ZOOS), the king of all gods. Zeus disguised himself as a swan to charm the beautiful Leda, a human. Leda then gave birth to two eggs. Helen hatched from the same egg as Clytemnestra (kly-tem-NESS-truh), Tyndareus' daughter. Helen's brothers, Castor and Pollux, hatched from the other egg. Pollux was also Zeus' son. Castor and Pollux were inseparable. But Clytemnestra was jealous of Helen's beauty. Tyndareus and Leda decided to keep the truth of Helen's birth a secret.

GROWING UP ROYAL

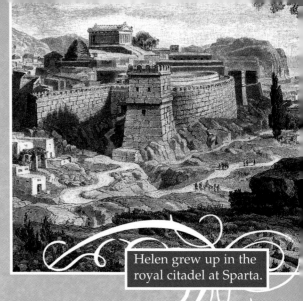

Helen grew up in the royal citadel at Sparta.

In Bronze Age Greece, royalty lived in high **citadels**. These walled palaces had beautiful views of water and hills. Helen grew up protected by rock walls. Summer days were hot, often over 100 degrees Fahrenheit (38 degrees Celsius). Fields grew thick with grapes and grains. Orchards burst with almond, fig, and olive trees. Farmers raised pigs, sheep, and goats.

As a royal princess, Helen was attended by maids-in-waiting. They served her food and helped her dress. They also kept her company as she visited temples and played among columned halls decorated with lively paintings. Helen learned to weave beautiful, soft cloth. Only the wealthy had time to create such rich fabrics.

Not many people in Bronze Age Greece could read or write. Boys received military training. Girls learned how to weave. Both boys and girls learned to sing and dance. Girls were married when they were 12 or 13 years old.

A DARK PROPHECY

Despite Helen's riches, the oracle at Delphi did not predict a happy life for Helen. The oracle was a shrine in northern Greece. A priestess oversaw the shrine and could look into the future. She said that Helen would start a war and ruin the city of Troy. Troy was about 275 miles (443 kilometers) northeast of Sparta, across the Aegean Sea.

As Helen grew older, stories of her beauty spread far and wide. King Tyndareus and Queen Leda watched Helen grow into a great beauty. The oracle's dreadful vision seemed too wicked to be true.

citadel — a fortress and command center of a city

QUEEN OF
Sparta

When Helen was old enough to get married, King Tyndareus invited men to compete for her hand. He declared that Helen and her new husband would reign as king and queen of Sparta. Many men knew of Helen's great beauty. They traveled long distances to compete for her hand in marriage and to see her with their own eyes. Gifts of livestock, grains, and gold were piled at Tyndareus' feet. The men competed in chariot races and displayed their athletic strength in sporting events.

Many men wanted to be Helen's husband. Tyndareus feared their competition would turn violent. He did not want to offend the suitors. To avoid conflict, Tyndareus made each man promise to defend whomever Helen married.

In the end, Tyndareus chose Prince Menelaus of Mycenae for Helen. Menelaus had wealth and power. He was the younger brother of the great Agamemnon (a-guh-MEM-nohn), the most powerful king in Greece. Helen's half sister, Clytemnestra, was married to King Agamemnon. The marriage of Helen and Menelaus would make for an even stronger political union.

Helen was a popular subject for Greek artists.

13

Menelaus and Helen married and became king and queen of Sparta. Visitors to their palace could hardly believe what they saw. Bronze, gold, silver, and ivory covered every surface. Helen soon gave birth to their daughter, Hermione (her-MY-oh-nee). The happy family lived in peace for many years.

THE VISITOR FROM TROY

When Paris arrived in Sparta, Menelaus welcomed and entertained him as an honored guest. In the palace's throne room, Menelaus hosted the fine banquet for which Helen had prepared so carefully. Paris and Menelaus drank mead together from golden goblets in an act of friendship. They enjoyed fine music and dancing.

Menelaus was already a rich and powerful prince before he married Helen.

Some historians believe Aphrodite (af-roh-DYE-tee), goddess of love, helped Paris charm Helen.

Paris was eager to meet Helen. He was young and handsome. He loved music and was a graceful dancer. Paris played music on his lyre to impress Helen. At the end of the night, Helen and Menelaus went to their quarters. Paris slept on thick animal skins on the stone floor of the hall.

HELEN IS MISSING

Not long after Paris' arrival, Menelaus left Sparta to attend his grandfather's funeral. Helen stayed behind to entertain their guest. Once Menelaus was gone, Helen could no longer ignore Paris' charms. Armed with her palace riches and a few servants, Helen left her home and family. She and Paris set sail for Troy. Helen ended her marriage to Menelaus the moment she stepped onto the boat.

Ancient Greeks and historians debate the reasons why Helen left Sparta with Paris. Did Aphrodite, the goddess of love, fan the flames of romance? Did Helen want to escape her marriage? Did Paris kidnap Helen? These questions remain unanswered. One thing was for sure — King Menelaus was furious.

Paris broke the laws of Greek hospitality. He dared to attack Menelaus after dining with him in friendship. This meant war, a risk Helen surely knew. The insulted Menelaus convinced his brother, Agamemnon, to lead an army against Troy.

Helen and Paris suffered a stormy journey but arrived in Troy unharmed. Paris' sister, Cassandra, warned that Helen would bring trouble to Troy. Only a few Trojans trembled with dread, knowing the risks of welcoming a stolen queen. Most citizens stared in awe, enchanted by Helen's great beauty. When Helen married Paris, Troy celebrated its lovely new princess.

Some historians argue that Paris kidnapped Helen. Others believe she left Sparta by choice.

THE GOLDEN APPLE

Paris was destined to play an important role in the Trojan War, long before the first blow was struck. When Paris was born, his mother had a nightmare. She dreamed her baby would cause the destruction of Troy.

The trouble continued many years later when all of the gods and goddesses gathered for a wedding. Eris, the goddess of strife, wasn't invited. In revenge for being snubbed, Eris threw a golden apple into the wedding feast. The apple was inscribed "For the Fairest." Three goddesses grabbed for the prize. Each assumed it was meant for her. They were Hera (HERE-uh), Athena (uh-THEE-nuh), and Aphrodite. They asked Zeus to choose which goddess deserved the apple.

Zeus didn't want to judge a beauty contest between three proud and powerful goddesses. He chose the handsome young mortal, Paris, for the job. Each goddess offered Paris a reward if he would choose her. Paris chose Aphrodite for her promise of Helen, the most beautiful woman in the world. Paris' choice set the wheels of war in motion.

Aphrodite (center), Hera (back left), and Athena (back right) asked Paris to choose which goddess was the fairest of all.

THE *Trojan* WAR

Greek heroes such as Odysseus (oh-DISS-ee-uhs) and Achilles (uh-KIL-eez) agreed to join Agamemnon's powerful army. These were the same men who promised to defend Helen's husband. Hoping to avoid war, Menelaus and Odysseus traveled to Troy ahead of the Greek army. They demanded Helen's return. They also asked the Trojans to pay heavy fines. The Trojans refused.

Helen watched many battles from the high walls of Troy.

THE WAR BEGINS

Agamemnon and his huge Greek army soon landed in Troy. Agamemnon wanted to help Menelaus, but he also wanted Troy's riches for himself. Hector, Paris' older brother, led the Trojan army. Hector was prepared to defend his city to the death. During the nine years that followed, neither side seemed close to victory. No matter how hard they tried, the Greeks couldn't break through Troy's strong walls.

Helen spent most of the war hiding in her chambers. She wove a large piece of purple cloth. The cloth showed the battles between the Greeks and Trojans. Iris, the messenger of the gods, appeared to Helen. She coaxed Helen outside to watch the battles. Helen tearfully draped her head with a veil. She went to the high wall of Troy, where she could see the battlefield below. King Priam, Paris' father, invited Helen to sit beside him. He asked her to point out the Greek heroes for him. In deep sadness, Helen named Odysseus, Achilles, and even Menelaus. Priam blamed the gods for bringing the war, but Helen blamed herself.

In the 10th year of the war, Paris challenged any member of the Greek army to a duel. The winner would claim Helen, and the war would end. Menelaus accepted the challenge. As the men battled, Aphrodite surrounded Paris in a cloud. She carried him away to safety. As a result, the war raged on.

"Father of my husband, dear and reverend in my eyes, would that I had chosen death rather than to have come here with your son, far from my bridal chamber, my friends, my darling daughter, and all the companions of my girlhood. But it was not to be, and my lot is one of tears and sorrow."

Helen to King Priam, in Homer's *The Iliad*

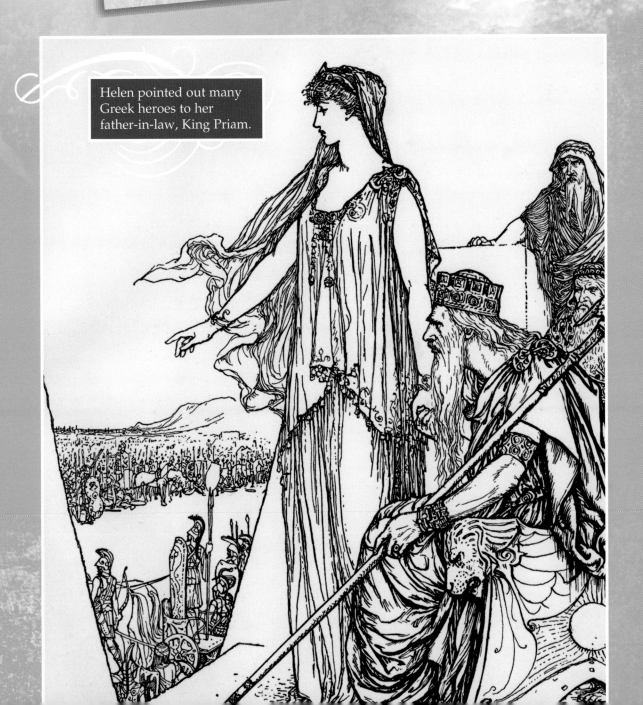

Helen pointed out many Greek heroes to her father-in-law, King Priam.

> "So, you are back from the battle. I wish you had died there, slain by that powerful man, my former husband!"
>
> Helen to Paris, after his rescue from the duel with Menelaus, in Homer's *The Iliad*

THE TROJAN HORSE

In the long and bloody war, many heroes were killed. Achilles killed Hector. Then Paris struck Achilles in the heel with an arrow. Achilles died from the wound. Finally, Paris himself was killed by an arrow. Helen then married Paris' brother, Deiphobus (dee-if-OH-bus).

In a plan to end the war, Menelaus, Odysseus, and the Greeks pretended to leave Troy. They built a huge wooden horse and hid inside its hollow belly. The Trojans found the horse looming outside the city gates. A Greek spy told them it was a gift for Athena, the goddess of war. The spy tricked them into believing the horse would protect their city. The Trojans pulled the gift inside and celebrated their victory. In the dark of night, the Greeks climbed out from inside the horse and destroyed Troy.

The Greeks waited until dark to climb out of the horse and attack the sleeping Trojan warriors.

Menelaus killed Deiphobus first. Then he rushed into Helen's chambers with his sword drawn, ready to cut her throat. At the sight of her beauty, he froze. Menelaus forgave Helen, and they reunited as husband and wife.

HELEN RETURNS TO SPARTA

After the fall of Troy, Helen and Menelaus set sail for Sparta. Their journey home was not easy. They suffered many storms and got lost in Egypt. When they finally landed in Sparta, Helen resumed her quiet life with Menelaus. She oversaw the marriage of their daughter, Hermione. During the wedding feast, the Spartans demanded answers about the war. Surviving Spartan warriors told stories of their pain and suffering. Their stories made Helen fear for her safety. She drugged the warriors' wine to make them laugh and forget their grief.

Menelaus considered killing Helen for her betrayal. Instead, they returned to Sparta as husband and wife.

Scientists believe the city of Troy was rebuilt eight times, one on top of the other like a stack of pancakes. Today only ruins of Troy remain.

CITY OF TROY

Troy was a great city during the Bronze Age. The city existed from about 3000 to 950 BC. Troy was one of the largest cities near the Aegean Sea. Stone walls, ditches, and wooden palisades protected the city. It had good access to the sea. During its peak, Troy covered 75 acres and had 5,000 to 7,500 citizens. The war that destroyed the city most likely happened between the years 1230 and 1180 BC.

Today the spot where Troy existed is located in northwest Turkey. Scientists have found evidence that supports Homer's stories. German **archaeologist** Heinrich Schliemann excavated the ruins of Troy in the 1870s. In his rush to uncover the city of the Trojan War, Schliemann destroyed some later structures. The site was also looted over the years.

A common artifact found from the layers of Troy was pottery. Experts can date the pottery. Images painted on the pots tell about life in Troy. Archaeologists have also uncovered jewels, goblets, and other artifacts.

AN *Eternal* *Subject* OF POETS

Helen's death remains a mystery. In some stories she died as an old woman. In one story, Helen was banished from Sparta when Menelaus died. She went to live with her friend Polyxo on the island of Rhodes. Polyxo's husband died during the Trojan war. She blamed Helen for her husband's death. In anger, Polyxo sent her servant girls to hang Helen from a tree. Homer suggested that Helen went with Menelaus to the Isles of the Blessed. There she lives eternally, forever young and beautiful.

When Homer wrote *The Iliad* and *The Odyssey* around 700 BC, writing had just been developed. Helen's story was already 500 years old. Some historic facts might have been preserved through storytelling. The story that survived is probably not completely true. Parts of the story changed as it was told over the years. The real details of Helen's life and the Trojan War may never be known.

Throughout history, many authors have written about Helen's life.

Since Homer first wrote about Helen, there have been many versions of her story. Other ancient Greek writers wrote about Helen. They portrayed Helen as either a villain or a victim, as vain and shallow, or as wise and grieving. In some versions of her story, Helen never went to Troy. One version says that Paris hid Helen in Egypt during the war. In another story, the goddess Hera decided to get even with Aphrodite for winning the golden apple. Hera created a false Helen to sail to Troy. She carried the real Helen safely to Egypt.

HELEN'S SHRINE

Though many see Helen's famous beauty as a curse, the Greek people never stopped worshipping her. Mirrors were carved with Helen's image. They even built a temple for Helen and Menelaus around 700 BC. It is simply called Helen's Shrine. People made pilgrimages and brought offerings to honor her. Girls visited the shrine to pray for beauty and happy marriages. Pregnant women visited to pray for healthy children. Today people still visit the site on a grassy hill, just a few miles south of modern Sparta. Helen's story continues to capture the imagination of poets and scholars.

Helen's story spread around the world. An Italian artist carved Helen's image into this mirror around 400 BC.

BRONZE AGE BEAUTY

Wealthy, royal Bronze Age women had many servants to help them decorate their bodies. Women wore elegant robes that draped to the floor. A large square of fabric folded and pinned at the shoulder could be cinched with a belt. Sandals covered their feet. Fabrics were dyed rich colors using herbs, plants, and vegetable skins. Weaving threads were drenched in scented olive oil to make the fabric soft and shiny. Only the rich could afford these fabrics.

Olive oil was also the base for perfumes scented with herbs, flowers, and spices. In the hot, dry landscape, women kept their skin soft by massaging it with perfumed olive oil until it glistened.

Bronze Age craftsmen were skilled metal artists. They created gold bracelets and anklets. Necklaces hung with medallions of precious stones. They also made dangling earrings and jeweled hair combs.

Women lined their eyelids with kohl, a black pastelike mascara. The paste was a mix of soot, frankincense, and burned almond shells. White skin was valued in Bronze Age Greece. In paintings, royal women have pale skin. They painted their arms and faces with white makeup.

Glossary

amethyst (AM-uh-thist) — a type of quartz crystal that is purple or violet and often is used as a gemstone in jewelry

ancient (AYN-shunt) — from a long time ago

archaeologist (ar-kee-AH-luh-jist) — a scientist who studies how people lived in the past

artifact (AR-tuh-fact) — an object used in the past that was made by people

Bronze Age (BRONZ AGE) — a period of history, before the introduction of iron, when bronze was commonly used to make tools and weapons; Greece experienced its Bronze Age from about 3000 to 1200 BC.

citadel (SIT-uh-del) — a fortress and command center of a city

lentil (LEN-tuhl) — the flat, round seed of a plant related to beans and peas; lentils are often cooked in soups.

lyre (LIRE) — a small, stringed, harplike instrument played mostly in ancient Egypt, Israel, and Greece

mead (MEED) — a wine-like drink made from water, honey, malt, and yeast

oracle (OR-uh-kuhl) — a place or person that a god speaks through; in myths, gods used oracles to predict the future or to tell people how to solve problems.

palisade (pal-uh-SAYD) — a fence of stakes built for defense

Read More

Fleischman, Paul. *Dateline: Troy.* Cambridge, Mass.: Candlewick Press, 2006.

Fontes, Justine, and Ron Fontes. *The Trojan Horse: The Fall of Troy: A Greek Legend.* Graphic Myths and Legends. Minneapolis: Graphic Universe, 2007.

Tracy, Kathleen. *The Life and Times of Homer.* Biography from Ancient Civilizations. Hockessin, Del.: Mitchell Lane, 2005.

Internet Sites

FactHound offers a safe, fun way to find educator-approved Internet sites related to this book.

Here's what you do:

1. Visit *www.facthound.com*
2. Choose your grade level.
3. Begin your search.

This book's ID number is 9781429623087.

FactHound will fetch the best sites for you!

Index